Takoyaki

25 Special Takoyaki Recipes you would Feel All the Way to your Toes

BY:

SOPHIA FREEMAN

HOME
FOOD
The best recipe

⋆ ⋆ ⋆ ⋆ ★ ★ ★ ★ ⋆ ⋆ ⋆ ⋆

Liability

This publication is meant as an informational tool. The individual purchaser accepts all liability if damages occur because of following the directions or guidelines set out in this publication. The Author bears no responsibility for reparations caused by the misuse or misinterpretation of the content.

Copyright

* * * ★ ★ ★ ★ ★ ★ ★ * * *

My gift to you!

Thank you, cherished reader, for purchasing my book and taking the time to read it. As a special reward for your decision, I would like to offer a gift of free and discounted books directly to your inbox. All you need to do is fill in the box below with your email address and name to start getting amazing offers in the comfort of your own home. You will never miss an offer because a reminder will be sent to you. Never miss a deal and get great deals without having to leave the house! Subscribe now and start saving!

Subscribe to the Newsletter!

Your email address | Subscribe

* * * ★ ★ ★ ★ ★ ★ ★ ★ * *

Table of Contents

Chapter I - Quick Takoyaki Recipes

ZZZZZZZZZZZZZZZZZZZZZZZZZZZZZZZZZZZZZZZZZZZZZZZZZZZZZZ

1) Shrimps Mix Octo Takoyaki Recipe

Preparation Time: 20 minutes

Makes: 2 to 3 servings

If you wish to try the combination of octopus and shrimps then this is the recipe for you. Try it; it will take just a few minutes to cook!

Ingredient List:

- Eggs - 2
- Cake flour - 2 cups
- Milk - 1 cup
- Water - ½ cup
- Dashi stock - 2 cups
- Cabbage (chopped) - 1 small
- Chives (chopped) - ½ cup
- Green onion (chopped) - ½ bunch
- Baby octopus - 1   c 500g
- Shrimps - 1 small pack
- Oil - 2 tablespoons

zzzzzzzzzzzzzzzzzzzzzzzzzzzzzzzzzzzzzzzzzzzzzzzzzzzzzz

* Replace 2 tablespoons of every 1 cup of plain flour with cornflour.

Methods:

Get a pan and add oil in it. Now cook baby octopus and shrimps in it. Let it turn light golden and take it off. Chop them both and keep aside.

On the other hand, mix cabbage, chives and green onions. In a separate bowl, mix eggs, flour, water and dashi stock. Now mix the chopped octopus and shrimps into this batter. Blend well.

Heat the Takoyaki pan and pour the batter in individual holes. Let it cook for 15 minutes. When done, it is ready to serve and enjoy!

2) Plain Takoyaki Recipe

Preparation Time: 20 minutes

Makes: 2 to 3 servings

If you do not want to fill anything in the balls then try this recipe which can be eaten as a side dish to any of your favorite dishes!

Ingredient List:

- Cake flour - 2 cups
- Dashi stock - 2 cups
- Eggs - 4

ZZZZZZZZZZZZZZZZZZZZZZZZZZZZZZZZZZZZZZZZZZZZZZZZZZZ

Methods:

Get a bowl and mix cake flour with dashi stock. Whisk the eggs in a separate bowl and add it to the mixture. Blend well.

Heat the Takoyaki pan and pour the batter in the individual holes. Let it cook for 12 minutes. When done, serve and enjoy the simple, delicious recipe!

3) Chicken Stock Mix Recipe

Preparation Time: 20 minutes

Makes: 2 to 3 servings

If you wish to have a taste of chicken in Takoyaki recipes then here is the perfect one for you with the chicken stock in it!

Ingredient List:

- Cooked baby octopus - 1
- Green onion - ½ bunch
- Ginger to taste
- Tempura crumbs - 1 small box

Batter:

- Cake flour - 2 cups
- Chicken stock - 2 cups
- Soy sauce - 1 tablespoon
- Sugar and salt to taste
- Bonito flakes - 1 cup
- Eggs - 2
- Skim milk (powder) - 2 tablespoons
- Baking powder - 2 tablespoons

Toppings:

- Honey or Takoyaki sauce (any of your choice)

ZZZZZZZZZZZZZZZZZZZZZZZZZZZZZZZZZZZZZZZZZZZZZZZZZZZZZ

Methods:

Get a bowl and chop the baby octopus with adding green onion in it. Add ginger to taste. Mix well.

Heat the pan lightly with adding chicken stock in it. Let it bowl. Add cake flour, soy sauce, sugar, salt, eggs, and skim milk. Tempura crumbs and baking powder to it. Cook for 10 minutes. Now add bonito flakes. Mix well.

Now heat the Takoyaki pan lightly and pour the mixture you made in step 2. Place the mixture over it which you made in step 1.

Let it cook for 10 minutes and then flip the balls. When done, dress it with your favorite toppings either honey or Takoyaki sauce to enjoy!

4) Takoyaki with Flakes

Preparation Time: 25 minutes

Makes: 2 to 3 servings

Missing the taste of yam in the Japanese dish? Well, here is the one for you which you can try for sure!

Ingredient List:

- Baby octopus (chopped) - 1
- Chives (chopped) - 1 bunch
- Eggs - 2
- Yam (chopped) - 2 cups
- Baking powder - 2 tablespoons
- Salt to taste
- Dashi stock - 1 cup
- Soy sauce - ½ tablespoons
- Ginger to taste
- Flakes for topping

ZZZZZZZZZZZZZZZZZZZZZZZZZZZZZZZZZZZZZZZZZZZZZZZZZZZ

Methods:

Get a bowl and add eggs, baking powder, dashi stock, soy sauce and salt in it. Mix well. Now add ginger.

Heat the Takoyaki pan and pour the batter in it. Place the baby octopus, chives, and yam on each hole. Let it cook for 10 minutes. Flip it over and cook for ten more minutes.

When done, place it on the plate and dress it with flakes on the balls. Enjoy the delicious meal!

5) Full Meal Takoyaki Recipe

Preparation Time: 25 minutes

Makes: 2 to 3 servings

A great dish for you to serve your family over the weekend. Invite your closed ones and try this amazing Japanese dish with them!

Ingredient List:

- Baby octopus - 1
- Mitsuba - 2 tablespoons
- Ginger to taste
- Batter:
- Cake flour - 2 cups
- Soy sauce - 1 tablespoon
- Chicken soup - 2 cups
- Milk - 2 cups
- Eggs - 2

Dipping sauce:

- Dashi stock - 2 cups
- Mirin - 1 tablespoon
- Soy sauce - 1 tablespoon
- Salt to taste

zzzzzzzzzzzzzzzzzzzzzzzzzzzzzzzzzzzzzzzzzzzzzzzzzzzzz

Methods:

Get a bowl and prepare the batter with adding cake flour, soy sauce, chicken soup, milk, and eggs together. Mix well.

Now chop the baby octopus and add mitsuba with ginger in a bowl. Blend both mixtures and heat the Takoyaki pan.

Pour the mixture into individual holes of the pan and let it cook for 20 minutes.

On the other hand, prepare the dipping sauce with mixing dashi stock with mirin and soy sauce. Mix well and add salt to it.

When the balls are ready, place them on the plate and pour the dipping sauce over it. Enjoy the delicious meal!

6) Dashi Stock Mix Recipe

Preparation Time: 25 minutes

Makes: 2 to 3 servings

A Japanese dish and no dashi stock in it? How is that even possible well, this is the best recipe with dashi stock to try!

Ingredient List:

- Dashi stock - 2 cups
- Soy sauce - 1 tablespoon
- Salt to taste
- Flour - 2 cups
- Boiled eggs - 3
- Green onions (chopped) - ½ bunch
- Ginger to taste

Topping:

- Takoyaki sauce - 1 tablespoon
- Bonito flakes - 1 cup
- Mayonnaise - 1 cup
- Aonori - 1 cup

ZZZZZZZZZZZZZZZZZZZZZZZZZZZZZZZZZZZZZZZZZZZZZZZZZZZ

Methods:

Get a bowl and mix dashi stock with soy sauce. Now add salt, flour, and ginger in it. Mix well.

Chopped the boiled eggs and add it to the mixture. Heat the Takoyaki pan and pour the batter in it with placing green onions on top of it. Let it cook for 15 minutes.

When cooked, place the balls on the plate. Dress it with Takoyaki sauce, bonito flakes, Aonori and at last with mayonnaise on it. When ready, serve and enjoy!

Chapter II - Sweet and Sour Takoyaki Recipes

ZZZZZZZZZZZZZZZZZZZZZZZZZZZZZZZZZZZZZZZZZZZZZZZZZZZZZZZ

7) Thick Honey Takoyaki Sauce

Preparation Time: 25 minutes

Makes: 2 to 3 servings

A simple sauce made with sugar, honey, and other ingredients will give you the best Takoyaki sauce you have ever had!

Ingredient List:

- Worcestershire sauce - 2 tablespoons
- Mentsuyu - ½ cup
- Ketchup - 2 tablespoons
- Sugar - 2 tablespoons
- Honey - 1 tablespoon

zzzzzzzzzzzzzzzzzzzzzzzzzzzzzzzzzzzzzzzzzzzzzzzzzzz

Methods:

Get a bowl and add Worcestershire sauce with sugar. Stir it well, so the sugar is dissolved in the sauce.

Add mentuyu with ketchup and honey. Blend well. When the mixture is thick, then it is ready to serve!

8) Simple Takoyaki Recipe

Preparation Time: 20 minutes

Makes: 2 to 3 servings

Try this basic recipe of Takoyaki if you have never tried it before. You will fall in love with this dish for sure.

Ingredient List:

- Takoyaki batter - 1 cup
- Egg - 1
- Water - ½ cup
- Baby octopus (chopped) - 1
- Scraps - ½ cup
- Mayonnaise as needed
- Takoyaki sauce as needed
- Dried green seaweed for garnishing

zzzzzzzzzzzzzzzzzzzzzzzzzzzzzzzzzzzzzzzzzzzzzzzzzzzz

Methods:

Get a bowl and add Takoyaki batter in it. Mix egg in it.

Add water, baby octopus, and scraps. Blend well. Heat the Takoyaki pan and pour the mixture in the individual holes. Let it cook for 15 minutes.

When done, serve with the dressing of Takoyaki sauce, mayonnaise and dried green seaweed for garnishing. Enjoy the simple and delicious dish!

9) Spinach Filled Takoyaki Recipe

Preparation Time: 20 minutes

Makes: 2 to 3 servings

The filling of spinach will make you mesmerized that how awesome the Takoyaki dish can be! There is no fat in this dish so make sure to try this!

Ingredient List:

- Baby octopus - 1 chopped
- Flour - 1 cup
- Water - ½ cup
- Dashi stock - 2 cups
- Eggs - 2
- Spinach (chopped) - 1 bunch

ZZZZZZZZZZZZZZZZZZZZZZZZZZZZZZZZZZZZZZZZZZZZZZZZZZZZ

Methods:

Get a bowl and add flour with water in it. Mix it well. Add dashi stock in it. Make sure there is no lump.

Beat the eggs in a separate bowl and keep it aside. Now mix spinach and octopus in the mixture you made in step 1.

Heat the Takoyaki pan. Make small balls out of the mixture in step 1 and dip the balls in the egg. Place them in the holes of the pan. Let it cook for 15 minutes. When done, serve and enjoy!

10) Takoyaki Recipe with Chili Sauce

Preparation Time: 25 minutes

Makes: 2 to 3 servings

You will be able to find the Takoyaki material from the market but how to make it delicious with your ingredients? Here is the recipe!

Ingredient List:

- Takoyaki material - 1 pack (small)
- Flour - 1 cup
- Egg - 1
- Water - ½ cup
- Chili sauce as needed
- Mayonnaise as needed

zzzzzzzzzzzzzzzzzzzzzzzzzzzzzzzzzzzzzzzzzzzzzzzzzzzzz

Methods:

Get a bowl and add the Takoyaki material. You will be able to find the material in the form of pack from the store.

Add flour, egg, and water in the material. Mix well. Heat the Takoyaki pan and pour the mixture in individual holes. Let it cook for 15 minutes. When done, serve on a plate with a dressing of mayonnaise and chili sauce over it. Enjoy the spicy Takoyaki dish!

11) Takoyaki Sauce with Different Spices

Preparation Time: 25 minutes

Makes: 2 to 3 servings

This is a recipe of sauce which is made of different spices. Mix the spices and taste the delicious sauce with any dish!

Ingredient List:

- Ketchup - 1 cup
- Teriyaki sauce - 2 tablespoons
- Mirin - 2 tablespoons
- Sugar - 2 tablespoons
- Onion powder - ¼ tablespoons
- Ginger powder - ½ tablespoons
- Garlic powder - ½ tablespoons

ZZZZZZZZZZZZZZZZZZZZZZZZZZZZZZZZZZZZZZZZZZZZZZZZZZZ

Methods:

Get a bowl and mix ketchup with sugar. Make sure the sugar is properly dissolved. Now add teriyaki sauce and mirin in it.

Blend well with adding onion powder, ginger powder and garlic powder in it. When done, the sauce is ready to be served with your favorite Takoyaki dish!

12) Ham and Cheese Takoyaki Recipe

Preparation Time: 20 minutes

Makes: 2 to 3 servings

Amazing combination of ham and cheese will compel you to prepare this dish again and again at home. You will love the mixture along with flakes on it!

Ingredient List:

- Flour - 1 cup
- Dashi powder - ½ tablespoons
- Egg - 1
- Soy sauce - ½ tablespoons
- Water - 1 cup

Filling:

- Ham (chopped) - 2 slices
- Cheese (chopped) - 1 small pack
- Mackerel Flakes - 1 handful
- Mayonnaise to taste

zzzzzzzzzzzzzzzzzzzzzzzzzzzzzzzzzzzzzzzzzzzzzzzzzzzzzzz

Methods:

Get a bowl and add egg, dashi powder, soy sauce, water and flour in it. Mix well.

Heat the Takoyaki pan and pour the batter in the individual holes. Now place the ham and cheese on the batter. Let it cook for 10 minutes. Flip the slips when cooked from the bottom. Cook it for 15 minutes.

When done, serve in a plate with mackerel flakes on it and mayonnaise. Enjoy!

Chapter III - Veggie and Meat Mix Takoyaki Recipes

ZZZZZZZZZZZZZZZZZZZZZZZZZZZZZZZZZZZZZZZZZZZZZZZZZZZZZ

13) Scrambled Egg Takoyaki Recipe

Preparation Time: 25 minutes

Makes: 2 to 3 servings

Try this recipe if you love the taste of eggs on every dish! It is mixed with shrimps and scrambled egg over it!

Ingredient List:

- Cake flour - 2 cups
- Baking powder - 1 tablespoon
- Eggs - 4
- Dashi stock - 2 cups
- Shrimps (chopped) - 1 small pack
- Ginger to taste
- Salt to taste
- Green onion (chopped) - ½ bunch
- Mayonnaise - ½ cup

ZZZZZZZZZZZZZZZZZZZZZZZZZZZZZZZZZZZZZZZZZZZZZZZZZZZZ

Methods:

Get a bowl and add cake flour with baking powder in it. Add dashi stock in it. You should have the shrimps boiled with chopping them into small pieces.

Add shrimps to the mixture. Blend well. Add ginger, salt, and mayonnaise in it. When done, heat the Takoyaki pan and pour the batter in the individual holes. Let it cook for 14 minutes.

Beat the eggs in a separate bowl with adding green onions to it. Pour the eggs mixture into the pan and let it cook for 5 minutes. When done, it is ready to serve and enjoy the meal!

14) Salmon Filled Takoyaki

Preparation Time: 25 minutes

Makes: 2 to 3 servings

The filling of salmon will make you fall in love with this recipe so do not miss out on this one for sure!

Ingredient List:

- Baking powder - 2 tablespoons
- Flour - 2 cups
- Salmon fish (chopped) - 1 lb.
- Salt to taste
- Dashi stock - 1 cup
- Soy sauce - ½ tablespoons
- Ginger to taste
- Chives (chopped) for garnishing

zzzzzzzzzzzzzzzzzzzzzzzzzzzzzzzzzzzzzzzzzzzzzzzzzzzzzzz

Methods:

Get a bowl and add flour, baking powder, salt, soy sauce and ginger in it. Mix well.

Add dashi stock to it. Heat the Takoyaki pan and pour the batter in it. Now add salmon fish in it and let it cook for 15 minutes.

When done, serve on a plate with garnishing chives on it.

15) Green Onion and Shrimp Mix Recipe

Preparation Time: 25 minutes

Makes: 2 to 3 servings

The combination of shrimp and green onion will make you forget all the other recipes which you ever loved! Try it now and do not miss out on this!

Ingredient List:

- Baking powder - 2 tablespoons
- Flour - 2 cups
- Salt to taste
- Eggs - 2
- Dashi stock - 1 cup
- Soy sauce - ½ tablespoons
- Ginger to taste
- Shrimps - 1 small pack
- Green onions (chopped) - a bunch

zzzzzzzzzzzzzzzzzzzzzzzzzzzzzzzzzzzzzzzzzzzzzzzzzzz

Methods:

Get a bowl and mix baking powder, flour, salt, eggs, soy sauce and ginger in it. Add dashi stock and blend well.

Heat the Takoyaki pan and pour the batter in it. Now place the shrimps with green onion over it. Let it cook for 15 minutes and when done, serve and enjoy the meal!

16) Potato Mix Recipe

Preparation Time: 25 minutes

Makes: 2 to 3 servings

Missing on potatoes? Then try this recipe and your craving for potatoes will be fulfilled for sure!

Ingredient List:

- Cake flour - 2 cups
- Dashi stock - 2 cups
- Potatoes (boiled, mashed) - 2
- Corn - 1 small can
- Eggs - 2
- Toppings:
- Takoyaki sauce - 2 tablespoons
- Ketchup as required

zzzzzzzzzzzzzzzzzzzzzzzzzzzzzzzzzzzzzzzzzzzzzzzzzzzzz

Methods:

Get a bowl and mix cake flour with dashi stock. Make sure there are no lumps in the batter. Now add mashed potatoes with corn in it.

Blend well. Heat the Takoyaki pan and pour the batter in it. Let it cook for 10 minutes. Beat the eggs in a bowl and pour it into the pan. Let it cook for another 10 minutes.

When done, place it on a plate with Takoyaki sauce over it or ketchup.

17) Cakey Takoyaki Balls

Preparation Time: 20 minutes

Makes: 2 to 3 servings

If you are fond of cakes then this is the best recipe which you can make. Make sure to keep the measurements accurate as it is the matter of sweet stuff!

Ingredient List:

- Cake flour - 1 cup
- Cocoa powder - 2 tablespoons
- Sugar (powdered) - 2 cups
- Milk - 1 cup
- Eggs - 2
- Vanilla essence - 1 tablespoon
- Baking powder - 1 tablespoon

Topping:

- Melted chocolate (any) - 1 small pack

ZZZZZZZZZZZZZZZZZZZZZZZZZZZZZZZZZZZZZZZZZZZZZZZZZZZZ

Methods:

Get a bowl and add cake flour, cocoa powder, sugar, milk, and eggs in it. Blend it well.

Add vanilla essence with baking powder. Mix it gently. Make sure there is no lump in the batter.

Heat the Takoyaki pan and pour the batter in individual holes. Let it cook for 15 minutes. When done, place it on the plate and pour the melted chocolate over each ball. Enjoy the delicious cakey Takoyaki recipe!

18) Takoyaki Recipe on Pan

Preparation Time: 20 minutes

Makes: 2 to 3 servings

If you wish to lose weight and want to have a flavor of meat as well then this is the best recipe to try!

Ingredient List:

- Cake flour -2 cups
- Baking powder - 1 tablespoon
- Katakuriko - 1 cup
- Eggs - 2
- Dashi stock - ½ cup
- Sugar and salt to taste
- Cabbage (chopped) - ½
- Baby octopus (boiled) - 1
- Leek (chopped) - 1 bunch
- Topping: Mayonnaise, Takoyaki sauce (any)

ZZZZZZZZZZZZZZZZZZZZZZZZZZZZZZZZZZZZZZZZZZZZZZZZZZZZ

Methods:

Heat a pan and add dashi stock in it. Let it boil.

Add cake flour, baking powder, katakuriko and eggs in a bowl. Mix well. Add sugar and salt to it.

Add the mixture to the pan and blend it slowly. Now add the cabbage, baby octopus and leek in it. Mix it properly and cover the pan for 10 minutes on low heat.

When done, serve it on a plate with any of your favorite toppings.

19) Takoyaki Sauce Recipe

Preparation Time: 25 minutes

Makes: 2 to 3 servings

An awesome sauce which is made of few ingredients will make you have it with all the meals which you will consume all week long!

Ingredient List:

- Oyster sauce - 2 tablespoons
- Worcestershire sauce - 2 tablespoons
- Honey - 2 tablespoons
- Ketchup - 1 tablespoon

zzzzzzzzzzzzzzzzzzzzzzzzzzzzzzzzzzzzzzzzzzzzzzzzzzzzzz

Methods:

Get a pan and add oyster sauce to it. Bring it to boil.

In a bowl, add Worcestershire sauce with honey and mix well. Add it to the pan and let it cook for 4 minutes. Add ketchup to it and stir well. Cook for five more minutes.

When done, pour it into an empty bottle or bowl, and you have the delicious Takoyaki sauce which you can take with any recipe!

Chapter IV - Takoyaki Recipes with Variations

ZZZZZZZZZZZZZZZZZZZZZZZZZZZZZZZZZZZZZZZZZZZZZZZZZZZZ

20) Octopus and Cabbage Filled Takoyaki Recipe

Preparation Time: 20 minutes

Makes: 2 to 3 servings

Follow the proper instructions of this recipe, and you will end up with the best recipe of Takoyaki for sure!

Ingredient List:

- Flour - 1 cup
- Oil for greasing
- Baking powder - 2 teaspoons
- Dashi stock - 1 tablespoon
- Eggs - 2
- Soy sauce - 1 tablespoon
- Salt and sugar to taste

Filling:

- Baby octopus (chopped) - 1 lbs.
- Spring onion - 2 tablespoons
- Pickled red ginger - 2 tablespoons
- Cabbage (chopped) - ½ cup
- Fish powder - 1 tablespoon

Topping:

- Mayonnaise - 2 tablespoons
- Takoyaki sauce - 2 tablespoons
- Fish powder to taste

ZZZZZZZZZZZZZZZZZZZZZZZZZZZZZZZZZZZZZZZZZZZZZZZZZZZZZZ

Methods:

Get a bowl and add flour, salt, and sugar with baking powder. Mix well. Keep it aside.

Get another bowl and whisk eggs in it with pouring soy sauce. Now add this mixture to the flour mixture. Add dashi stock to it and blend well.

Brush oil on the Takoyaki pan on the individual holes. Set it over the top of the stove on low heat. Pour the batter into the individual holes. Now top it off with onions, baby octopus, red ginger and cabbage with fish powder. When the bottom part is cooked, flip each set. Let it cook for 10 minutes. When done, take it out and place it on a plate.

Dress it with Takoyaki sauce, mayonnaise with fish powder on it. Now it is ready to serve and enjoy!

21) Sweet And light Takoyaki

Preparation Time: 25 minutes

Makes: 2 to 3 servings

A light flavor of sweet which you want to have after every dinner. This is the perfect recipe for you to make over the weekend and enjoy all week long!

Ingredient List:

- Milk - 2 cups
- Eggs - 2
- Chocolate (any) - 1 small pack
- Cubed apple - 1
- Peanuts (crushed) - 1 cup
- Icing sugar - 1 cup

ZZZZZZZZZZZZZZZZZZZZZZZZZZZZZZZZZZZZZZZZZZZZZZZZZZZZ

Methods:

Get a bowl and mix milk with eggs. Now add the apples with peanuts in it. Blend well.

On the other hand, crush the chocolate pieces and add it to the batter.

Heat the Takoyaki pan and pour the mixture in it. Let it cook for 15 minutes. When done, dress it with icing sugar and enjoy the crunchy Takoyaki balls.

22) Taco Meat Recipe

Preparation Time: 25 minutes

Makes: 2 to 3 servings

Wish to have light but cheesy Takoyaki recipe? Here is the perfect one for you to try!

Ingredient List:

- Taco meat - 1 cup
- Shredded cheese - ½ cup
- Shumai wrappers - 1 small pack
- Water - 2 cups
- Mexican tacos - 1 small pack

zzzzzzzzzzzzzzzzzzzzzzzzzzzzzzzzzzzzzzzzzzzzzzzzzzz

Methods:

You can pick the favorite meat you want for the filling of Takoyaki ball. It can be made of chicken or beef. Prepare that upon your choice.

Dip the wrappers into the water so that any extra flour is removed. Now add the meat filling in the wrapper. Make a shape of a ball.

On the other hand, heat the Takoyaki pan and add balls in the individual holes. Spread shredded cheese over it with tacos on it for crunch. Let it cook for 12 minutes. When cooked, it is ready to serve and enjoy!

23) Nutella Filled Takoyaki Recipe

Preparation Time: 20 minutes

Makes: 2 to 3 servings

If you love Nutella then this recipe is for you! So do not miss out on the delicious recipe. You will surely love the taste with the Takoyaki touch!

Ingredient List:

- Self-rising flour - 1 cup
- Caster sugar - 1/3 cup
- Baking powder - ½ tablespoons
- Egg - 1
- Milk - 1 cup
- Melted butter - ½ cup
- Nutella jar - 1 small

zzzzzzzzzzzzzzzzzzzzzzzzzzzzzzzzzzzzzzzzzzzzzzzzzzzz

Methods:

Get a bowl and add sugar, baking powder and flour. Mix well.

Whisk the egg and milk in a separate bowl and then add it to the flour mixture. Add melted butter to it and blend well. Make sure the batter is without any lumps.

Heat the Takoyaki pan and pour the batter in individual holes. Let it cook for 5 minutes and when the top is a little firm, pop it from the top and add a tablespoon of Nutella in each ball. Let it cook for another 10 minutes.

When done, it is ready to serve and enjoy!

24) Bananas Tops Recipe

Preparation Time: 25 minutes

Makes: 2 to 3 servings

A delicious sweet Takoyaki recipe which you would want to try and keep it safe for the whole week to have it after every meal!

Ingredient List:

- Pancake mix - 1 box
- Eggs - 2
- Water - ¼ cup
- Bananas (sliced) - 2
- Maple syrup - 2 tablespoons

ZZZZZZZZZZZZZZZZZZZZZZZZZZZZZZZZZZZZZZZZZZZZZZZZZZZ

Methods:

Get a bowl and mix the pancake mix with eggs and water. Beat it well until there are no lumps in the batter.

Heat the Takoyaki pan and pour the batter in it. Let it cook for 15 minutes and when the balls start to rise, take it off. Place the balls on the plate and dress it with banana and maple syrup on it. Enjoy when ready!

25) Mixed Veggie Takoyaki Recipe

Preparation Time: 20 minutes

Makes: 2 to 3 servings

Don't feel like cooking today? Here is the quick recipe which you can enjoy tonight!

Ingredient List:

- Eggs - 2
- Mixed vegetables - 1 small pack
- Salt to taste
- Vegetable oil - ½ tablespoons
- Onion (chopped) - 1
- Garlic (chopped) - 1 clove
- Rice (boiled) - 1 cup
- Chicken cube - 1
- Ketchup - 3 tablespoons

zzzzzzzzzzzzzzzzzzzzzzzzzzzzzzzzzzzzzzzzzzzzzzzzzzzz

Methods:

Get a pan and add vegetable oil in it. Now add the mixed vegetables and cook them until tender. Add salt to it. Mix well.

Add onion, garlic and chicken cube. Let it cook. You should have boiled rice in a bowl. When the mixture is ready, add it to the boiled rice bowl. Blend it well.

Heat the Takoyaki pan. Beat eggs in a separate bowl. Make small balls out of the mixture and dip them in the egg by placing each ball in the individual holes of the pan. Let it cook for 10 minutes.

When done, serve it with the dressing of ketchup and enjoy!

About the Author

A native of Albuquerque, New Mexico, Sophia Freeman found her calling in the culinary arts when she enrolled at the Sante Fe School of Cooking. Freeman decided to take a year after graduation and travel around Europe, sampling the cuisine from small bistros and family owned restaurants from Italy to Portugal. Her bubbly personality and inquisitive nature made her popular with the locals in the villages and when she finished her trip and came home, she had made friends for life in the places she had visited. She also came home with a deeper understanding of European cuisine.

Freeman went to work at one of Albuquerque's 5-star restaurants as a sous-chef and soon worked her way up to head chef. The restaurant began to feature Freeman's original dishes as specials on the menu and soon after, she began to write e-books with her recipes. Sophia's dishes mix local flavours with European inspiration making them irresistible to the diners in her restaurant and the online community.

Freeman's experience in Europe didn't just teach her new ways of cooking, but also unique methods of presentation. Using rich sauces, crisp vegetables and meat cooked to perfection, she creates a stunning display as well as a delectable dish. She has won many local awards for her cuisine and she continues to delight her diners with her culinary masterpieces.

* * * * ★ ★ ★ ★ ★ * * *

Author's Afterthoughts

I want to convey my big thanks to all of my readers who have taken the time to read my book. Readers like you make my work so rewarding and I cherish each and every one of you.

Grateful cannot describe how I feel when I know that someone has chosen my work over all of the choices available online. I hope you enjoyed the book as much as I enjoyed writing it.

Feedback from my readers is how I grow and learn as a chef and an author. Please take the time to let me know your thoughts by leaving a review on Amazon so I and your fellow readers can learn from your experience.

My deepest thanks,

Sophia Freeman

Subscribe to the Newsletter!

Your email address   Subscribe

https://sophia.subscribemenow.com/

* * * ★ ★ ★ ★ ★ ★ ★ * * *

Printed in Dunstable, United Kingdom